more praise for
## *even this page is white*

"*even this page is white* is a provocative meditation on what it means to grow up anything other than white in Canada, tackling institutional racism and sexual identity from a unique viewpoint, all delivered with astute observation and trenchant insight."

—Rollie Pemberton, former Edmonton Poet Laureate

"Vivek Shraya radically centres radiant darkness in *even this page is white*. In and around and between the lines I see multi-dimensional reflections of myself; all the possibilities of my becoming. Beasts are everywhere, outside and in, and Vivek's words root my courage to face them in love-a-lutionary soil."

—d'bi.young anitafrika, Canadian Poet of Honour

"With her debut poetry collection, Shraya applies her keen intelligence and awareness of positionality to white privilege and systemic racism. The book's accessibility and attention to everyday racism will undoubt-edly elicit comparisons to Claudia Rankine's
*Citizen: An American Lyric.*"

—*PRISM international*

ARSENAL PULP PRESS
Suite 202 – 211 East Georgia St.
Vancouver, BC V6A 1Z6
Canada
*arsenalpulp.com*

The publisher gratefully acknowledges the support of the Canada Council for the Arts and the British Columbia Arts Council for its publishing program, and the Government of Canada (through the Canada Book Fund) and the Government of British Columbia (through the Book Publishing Tax Credit Program) for its publishing activities.

The author gratefully acknowledges the support of the Toronto Arts Council for the writing of this book.

"indian" was published in *The Ethnic Aisle* (February 2016) and "prologue / gestation" was published in *This Magazine* (March/April 2016).

Cover photograph by Alejandro Santiago
Cover and text design by Oliver McPartlin

Printed and bound in Canada

Library and Archives Canada Cataloguing in Publication:

Shraya, Vivek, 1981-, author
Even this page is white / Vivek Shraya.

Poems.
ISBN 978-1-55152-641-6 (paperback)

I. Title.

PS8637.H73E84 2016    C811'.6    C2016-901425-8

**even this page is white**
vivek shraya

ARSENAL PULP PRESS • VANCOUVER

for anyone who has lost
a friend
from saying the word
race

*vivek—*
*the page is always white*
*because it is a void—*
*"a voidance"—*
*until ink cometh to*
        *make it right—*
*and blankness is destroyed—*
*and black words dance.*

—george elliott clarke
(december 2015)

────────────

*if whiteness gains currency*
*by being unnoticed*
*then what does it mean*
*to notice whiteness?*

—sara ahmed

# contents

white dreams

*to be anything in this world, you need to get a white person to like you.*

—scaachi koul

## white dreams

i have white dreams
billboards magazines
mighty praise accolades
top 10 lists and top 10 hits

so i climb dodge boulders
earn blisters but even
the top of the mountain
is white

i have a white boy i top
i dream on his long body
as his past bodies have long
built upon mine but when i cum

on the dip in his spine
even the colour of my pleasure
is white. body you betray me
the only brown i make

for sewer but for him
for him my brown body
makes white makes nice
if my cum was brown

would he still eat it? from my core
i seek courage
but even my bones
are white

is it my skin that betrays
this skeleton? i pray
for answers for my dreams
hunched back dim light

blue ink blank paper knelt over
wept over now i grasp why thirty-four
years of praying through writing
awoke no god

even
this page
is white
so i protest this page

mask it with words
words about being brown
about my mother
my motherland

but even these words
have white
dreams billboards magazines
crystal trophies

because what are words
without dreams
and what is a dream
if it is not white?

## indian

podium mic on
remind them
this land is not ours
heads nod hands clap
feet fixed
are you even in the room?

once my mother accidentally drove near a reserve
the only time i have seen her afraid hit gas pedal
strange to be indian and the sound of car locks
to be synonymous with *indians*

is acknowledgement enough?
*i acknowledge i stole this*
but i am keeping it social justice
or social performance
what would it mean to digest you and yours and
blood and home and land and minerals and trees and dignities
and legacies
to really honour no
show gratitude no
word for partaking in violence in progress

last year baltimore intersection black man
approaches once again a finger reaches for car
lock except this time the finger
is mine.

**amiskwacîwâskahikan**

so preoccupied
with my own
displacement
didn't notice
i was displacing

                you

gave myself
a white name
adam in place of
*divek civic ribbit*
didn't bother to learn

                yours

**fair**
*for shamik*

your second mother
when you had half a father
my arm ever wrapped around your shoulder
rolled macaroni burritos for your dinner
knock knock jokes for your laughter

but when they asked you
*why are you so much darker*
*than your brother* called you the n word
lingered for an answer
all i did was bask.

**talc**

*go get it*
under bathroom sink rusted pipes
        behind vaseline body cream
beside evergreen hair oil
        avon talcum powder turn the lid
smell forest and future
        offer it to my mother she snows
my face saffrons my lips
        her revlon *just for special events*
in my finest i was white
        and i was woman.

**antaryami**

he passes by doesn't notice
your palms pushed together your palms

wiping cement to collect dust dirt
he stepped on to wipe over your face

you used to sing *he is the indweller
of my heart* you used to say

he likes the white followers more
i was ten and attentive

if this is true at least i'm canadian
a psyche so trampled

to accept that even our guru
our god prefers white over us.

**even this stage**

        voted *most annoying voice* in junior high
i knew you meant most faggot voice
        even when the yearbook committee changed
        the category to *most unique voice* also voted

        *most talented singer* most talented faggot
i'll take it earned it singing madonna disney
        at assemblies *a whole new world*
        of pop requires a song to be sing-alongable

if you can't sing with me like me
the song doesn't echo has no value
what if i don't sound like you? a voice
molded by ragas and my mother's

later roused by r&b riffs and emotion
the closest semblance on radio to indian
classical devotion whitney taught me
a new way to pray but when i open

my mouth i'm told *restraint sing less*
*fewer* notes file this advice alongside other
efforts to render my voice pleasing
palpable reduce inflection lower pitch

what if i don't sound like you? what if
i don't look like you? bleached my hair
learned guitar covered pearl jam u2
listeners still say *eastern influences*

reviews say vocals are *irritating acquired taste*
most annoying less fewer restrain reduce lower
sometimes i forget that i know
how to sing.

## raji

*you have a twin* worst thing to tell a queen
*his name is raji* i despise him already
*who?* i ask avert my eyes
i guess *he is brown and tall*
no one says *and queer*
no one needs to

i am told of my twin often with a snicker a secret
joke on both of us
hope we never meet

i recognize my twin across the central academic building hallway
so gangly his wrists scrape the floor giraffe neck
rusty streaks in his mushroom haircut
we pretend not to notice each other
betrayed by the presence
of the other

he knows the precise strain and witchery to refashion
deviance flamboyancy as extraordinary
why would he take
this away from me?

so accustomed to being token
his arrival obsoleted me

two weeks later i'm told *by the way raji can't stand you*
two brown faggots distantly loathing each other
because how else can we liberate the hurt
from being brown and queer in a dirt city
that hates us so hard
that even one word *twin*
tells us that there isn't enough space
for both

dear raji sorry for not recognizing you as my brother
admiring you as my sister.

**birth certificate says m**

*man* became punctuation in the nineties
man seizing the last word
       *how's it going man*

my brother an ambassador of this trend
i asked him not to *man* with me
       *what's your problem man*

forever forgiven under front of sibling rivalry
but for one fight my remorse endures
       *chill man*

thick cordless phone in my hand
beat his face with it
       *how many times have i told you i am not a man*

beat

        *don't*

beat

        *fucking*

beat

        *call me*

beat

        *man*

his face spilling
fear and somehow
      love.

**cycle of violence**

without seeing a white cock i knew
my teenage penis was too dark
       no patch of my brown body is safe
from white sovereignty not even between my legs

without means to under my over colour
i warned potential lovers:
       *i nicknamed it "oprah"*
shifting shame into a joke about a black woman.

whitespeak

## a lover's bookshelf

| | | | |
|---|---|---|---|
| tolstoy | knowles | belloc | stoker |
| woolf | lerner | camus | adler |
| shakespeare | diamond | rigby | toole |
| graves | wallace | eggers | franzen |
| salinger | shrag | hemingway | nabokov |
| brontë | austen | orwell | o'neill |
| cocteau | pushkin | findley | shteyngart |
| sedaris | hecht | hall | trudeau |
| norris | walter | doyle | thomson |
| dostoyevsky | vonnegut | kerouac | jacobs |
| hamilton | ondaatje | kundera | didion |
| wilde | hébert | harrison | lane |
| steinbeck | irving | mousnier | updike |
| fowles | davies | dickens | eugenides |
| adams | hosseini | bök | krauss |
| marquez | lee | õnnepalu | basilières |
| golding | white | thurber | heti |
| king | beatty | baldwin | chabon |
| gogol | maclennan | buckley | coupland |
| kundera | le guin | marquez | gopnik |
| mccarthy | boyden | diaz | atwood |
| tolkien | mahadevan | smith | munro |
| l'engle | doctor | chandler | rakoff |
| goldman | francis | dahl | saunders |
| twain | bergen | dunn | shields |
| rowling | bryson | richards | sebald |
| gravestock | le carré | bergman | klein |
| winterson | dickens | reid | macmillan |
| bechdel | conrad | allen | mowat |
| mccartney | richler | hornby | mantel |
| hollinghurst | shields | shields | brown |

## yellowface

short answer: rejected
under my real name
put yi-fen's name on

a strategy
successful for me
this is the best american

i'm persistent
i did briefly consider
to make yi-fen a persona

nothing came of it.

## what pride sounded like june 24, 2015

*for jennicet, a hero not a heckler*

release all lgbtq in detention centres

hold on a
second no          stop the torture and abuse          shhh shhhh shhhh
no no no no                                             shhhh shhh shhhh
no no no no    of trans women in detention centres     shhhhhhh   shhhhh
no no you're                                            shhhh shhh shhhh
in my house          i'm a trans woman                 shhh shhhh shhh
you're not                                              shhhh shhh shhhh
going to          i'm tired of the abuse                shhhh shh shhhhh
get a good                                              shh shhhh booo booo
r e s p o n s e    i'm tired of the violence            booo boooo booo
from me by                                              booo booo booo booo
interrupting   i'm tired of the violence we're facing   shame shhh shhhh
me like                                                  shhhh shhh shhhh
this shame          not one more deportation             shhhh this is not for
on you you                                               you it's for all of us
s h o u l d n' t      release all lgbtq                  shhhh shhh shhhh
be doing                                                 shhhh shhh shhhh
this can             stop the abuse                      shhhh shhh shhh
we escort                                                enough shhh shhhh
this person         not one more deportation             take her out shhhh
out you                                                  shut up shhhh shhh
can either          not one more deportation             shhh shh shhh shhh
stay and                                                 shhh shhh shhhhh
be quiet or         not one more deportation
we'll have
to take you         not one more deportation
out

                    not one more deportation

                    not one more deportation

**54,216 signed petition
to ban kanye west from playing pan am games closing ceremony**

not canadian
big mouth
arrogant
egotistical
asshole
insult to music
idiot
horrible
pretentious
pathetic human
being
billionaire
smarmy
message is
satanic
disgusting
reprehensible
thinks he's a
"god"
bad influence
nasty wife
sucks balls
retard
parasite
everything
wrong with
society music
and culture
disgusting

dick
pussy ass bitch
doesn't deserve
anyone's
respect
prick
unethical
douchebag
disgrace to
music
worst
no talent hack
disgrace to
humans
makes me want
to puke
worst human
being on earth
disgrace to the
human race
acts like a
spoiled toddler
self righteous
loser who should
be wiped off the
face of the earth
likes fish dicks
fool
terrible musician

insulted a man
in a wheelchair
convicted
criminal
embarrassment
to the words
artist, musician,
sane person
thinks only about
himself
foul language
offense to music
pop culture and
humanity
doesn't respect
other artists
untalented wife
childish
behaviour
bully
poor loser
twit
needs a reality
check
an ego the size
of an elephant's
arse
hypocrite
arrogant ass

racist
homophobe
punk
disgrace
lowlife with no
class
mediocre ego
poor excuse for
a human and a
musician
imposter
worse than
ebola and hitler
not a very nice
person
talentless hack
scumbag
garbage
dumbass
irrelevant
sucks and blows
pompous
no talent bum
a plague on the
music industry
disrespectful
overpaid
joke
too expensive

massive ego
hippo assed
porn slut wife
not professional
clown
sore loser
racist bigot
money
obsessed
fat ass wife
retarded looking
kid
needs to be
knocked down a
peg
garbage
incarnate
needs to learn
when it's time to
fuck off
big mouth piece
of shit noron
married to a 2 bit
whore
no brains
connected to a
kardashian
turd sandwich
american

selfish ass
sucks at singing
nob gobling
thunder punt
epitome of
horrible people
no manners
caused trouble
many times
will turn the
games into a
racism issue
makes me
ashamed to be
human
clown prince
stinky
of entertainers
exemplifies poor
sportsmanship
shallow
delusional
fucking knob
poor public
behaviour
epitome of a
poor sport
immature brat
ass hat

butchered
"bohemian
rhapsody"
stands for greed
very self-
centered
incapable of
playing a
musical
instrument
not a musician
a lack of humility
and grace
awful
inflated ego
ungrateful idiot
tool
rude
narcissistic fraud
jerk
total waste of
human dna
useless waste of
skin
high lord of
douchebag
ignorant
worse than a
bag of dicks

biggest d-bag i
have ever seen
waste of oxygen
dildo
not deserving
s.o.b.
none of the
qualities we
admire in the
human race
not be allowed
near a crowd of
human beings
disgraces to
fairness and
respect
an insult to
everybody
poor role model
makes bad
music
represents the
most pretentious
guy in the world
worst example
no talent period
spoiled
cannot sing
talentless

**#oscars2016**

racist to whites
black actors did not deserve

why classify people
we are accepted

he's too black
minorities everywhere

he's not very good
but he's black

give a good performance
be patient

wish I were african american
people don't bash them

hardest to be a woman
thousands haven't won

people are crying
sitting complaining

go do something
that subject is boring.

**miley, what's good?**

if you want to make it about race
don't make it about yourself
say *this*

nicki is not too kind
not very polite
there's a way you speak to people

i'm a white pop star
i know the statistics
i know what's going on in the world.

**how to talk to a white person**

*...i think one has to even abandon the phrase 'ally' and understand that you are not helping someone in a particular struggle; the fight is yours.*

—ta-nehisi coates

**saraswati**

words   can i trust you to say what
words   have struggled to say
words   can you bridge over where
words   have sunk slammed rock from rift
words   ever my raft yet
words   punctured this craft how odd to look to

words   the refuge and the dagger

words   have i never asked you what you want
words   have i never let you do the talking
*words*   *are what got us here*—a lie
words   what would you say if i didn't interfere what
words   would you use to say *pain* and have
words   cease and provoke listening.

## eraser

*I will not make this about race.*
*I will not make this about race.*
*I will not make this about race.*
*I will not make this about race.*
*I will not make this about race.*

*I will not make believe.*
*I will not make believe.*
*I will not make believe.*
*I will not make believe.*
*I will not make believe.*

*I will not bring my race to work.*
*I will not bring my race to work.*
*I will not bring my race to work.*
*I will not bring my race to work.*
*I will not bring my race to work.*

*I will not bring my race to school.*
*I will not bring my race to school.*
*I will not bring my race to school.*
*I will not bring my race to school.*
*I will not bring my race to school.*

*I will not share my race online.*
*I will not share my race online.*
*I will not share my race online.*
*I will not share my race online.*
*I will not share my race online.*

*Race is a choice not a construct.*
*Race is a choice not a construct.*
*Race is a choice not a construct.*
*Race is a choice not a construct.*
*Race is a choice not a construct.*

## count the brown people

1n y0ur 1tunes tw1tter
feed fr1end c1rcle

sex l1fe café classr00m
textb00k ne1ghb0urh00d

0n the walls 0f y0ur art
gallery tv screen l1sts cred1ts

at y0ur galas dance
d1nner h0use

h0l1day part1es staff
meet1ng

　　　　1 am capt1ve c0unt1ng search1ng
　　　　a cl0ck with a sec0nd hand stuck

brown life is an unbroken bearing of the weight and hollow of the active
absence of brown life.

**#notallwhitepeople**

i don't know your story
this is true

you are a good person
sterling intentions
golden heart
extra mile

your parents laboured
you grew up poor
picked on and kicked out
haunted by loss

many truths can be true
at once you can be all
the above
and you can be racist.

*because race is constructed as residing in people of colour, whites don't bear the social burden of race…we move easily through our society without a sense of ourselves as racialized. race is for people of colour to think about—it is what happens to "them"—they can bring it up if it is an issue for them (although if they do, we can dismiss it as a personal problem, the race card, or the reason for their problems). this allows whites much more psychological energy to devote to other issues and prevents us from developing the stamina to sustain attention on an issue as charged and uncomfortable as race.* —dr robin diangelo

## a dog named lavender

are you staring at me because
are you not looking at me because
you don't like me because
you don't desire me because
you desire me only because
i don't like myself because
i wish i was like you
am i safe here
where are the others like me
there are no others like me
i was not considered because
i was only considered because
why would you say that
i thought you cared about me
did you say that because
do i respond
how do i respond in a way that you will hear me
how do i respond without making you angry
or uncomfortable
can i be ok with not responding
why doesn't someone else respond
i shouldn't have said anything
are you ignoring me because i responded

there has to be another explanation
maybe i am making this up
maybe i am too sensitive
maybe i am too defensive
maybe i am undesirable
not everything is because
i can't assume the worst
of course i am safe here
of course there are others like me here
you probably haven't seen someone like me
i just need to work harder
you don't know how to think about this
you don't mean what you said
of course you care about me
of course you will hear me
maybe it's good for you to be uncomfortable
maybe i'm better off in the long run
what would i think of if i wasn't thinking about this
a dog named lavender
a home in idaho
a book about landscapes
what would I make if I wasn't thinking about this
who could i be if i wasn't thinking about this?

## the truth about the race card

is that even before i knew what it meant
i knew not to play it refused

to spin brown into excuse let it hold me back
believed you when you said we are the same

blamed my parents and camouflaged to prove
you right no wonder you couldn't see me

people who said *racism* were whiny or lazy
and i was neither

but there's no worth for my work no toll for my toil
when you hold the cards keys gavels

unravelled, brown is not a barrier you are
and when you say *don't play the race card*

you mean *don't call me white.*

*you are so articulate*

i had to
      ☐ inherit a lighter shade
         from my mom's side
      ☐ be born in Canada
      ☐ be designated male

dad had to
      ☐ work three jobs
         sold vacuums door to door
         *fly on your magic carpet*
         *back from where you came*

to work three jobs he had to
      ☐ give his time off to sleep
         instead of knowing me

mom had to
  ☐ be dad
  ☐ stay awake alert
  ☐ be a bedtime story and work
  ☐ make my teeth less crooked
  ☐ make sure i could go to university
    so i would have money
    not have to be shift working
    unfamiliar like dad

i had to
  ☐ reject mom and dad's dreams
    of becoming an engineer
    a profession
  ☐ major in english

     for you to hear me.

**conversation with white friends:**
**sara quin amber dawn rae spoon dannielle owens-reid**
*because i still believe in the value of dialogue*
*and because white people listen to white people*

**when did you realize being white gave you privilege?**
**what was that experience like?**

sq: my awareness of racism and my whiteness started in junior high school. our behaviour as kids—the way we talked, dressed, fought, expressed ourselves—was scrutinized on an entirely different scale depending on the race of the student. i was experiencing white privilege first-hand and knew then that it was unfair.

ad: when i was in fourth grade my friend thi and i were spending another lunch break in our teacher's office. both thi and i had served lunch break detention before, had been sent to the principal's office, and were regularly called "bad," "stupid," and "lazy" by teachers. we were both poor. both of us were surviving violence at home. during this particular detention, thi tried to flee the office. the teacher grabbed her by the arm and physically dragged her back to her chair. i remember thinking that the teacher would never touch me like that. it took me many years to figure out that it was my whiteness that protected me.

dor: once i started getting involved in queer spaces and met queer people of colour who had such drastically different experiences from mine, i was like "whoa, whoa, whoa" and started to examine my understanding. i remember my friend andre telling me about the challenges of being gay in a black family. as time went on, i would think about his story all the time, and then i met you and you had all of this knowledge that you explained in such a cool and easy-to-understand way. i had never really heard the word "privilege" but once you were explaining it so clearly, i was able to look back on my life experiences and see that you were right and it was legit. and i was so happy to have a word to define it. i've always felt a little lost in talking about racism until i met you because i didn't have the ability to say, "it's going to be harder for someone with immigrant parents. it doesn't mean they can't have the good life, it just means they'll have more obstacles, because people look at their parents, hear an accent, and assume a bunch of shit."

**in instances where your white privilege has been
highlighted, how do you manage any defensiveness?**

ad: i listen. i let the person know i've heard them. i might ask the
person if they need anything from me in the moment. i might offer
an apology. i thank the person for taking the time to educate me.
i let the person know that i will think more about what they said.
i debrief with other white people. sometimes, depending on the
situation, i debrief and discuss with people of colour with their
consent. i don't expect any of this to feel comfortable.

rs: the *toronto star* did a cover article on "they" as a singular pronoun
and decided to put a photo of me on the front page. when the article
came out, i found out that the paper had mainly interviewed white
people who use the pronoun. elisha lim requesting "they" as a
pronoun from *xtra* and the boycott that happened until that paper
started using it for people was a huge part of my own coming out
as agender. elisha brought up the exclusion of poc folks from the
article with me. i had a moment of feeling defensive, and also i felt
like i had really let them down. it felt like being wrong, and i wanted
to do anything i could not to be wrong or to get out of the situation.
i tried to remember what it's like to be on the other side of that
kind of space-taking, and i tried to keep it to a minimum. i wrote a
statement on tumblr about the exclusion and shared it in the same
spaces i had shared the article.

**how do you reconcile being white with the history of colonization by white people in north america?**

ad: i doubt the small acts i currently do can be called reconciliation. in my working life, i read aboriginal writing, both scholarly and literary. i include aboriginal authors in my curriculum. when i have voting power as to how guest speaker funds are spent where i teach, i put forward the names of aboriginal authors. when i receive author payments from work where i've written about sex work, i designate a modest percentage of that payment to the missing and murdered memorial march committee in vancouver.

rs: the final report of the truth and reconciliation commission defines reconciliation as an ongoing process of establishing and maintaining respectful relationships. reading that really impacted me because of my own history with being the victim of abuse. it raised my awareness of the fact that i am approaching relationships with indigenous people in canada from the side of the abusers and the people who benefit from that cultural genocide. it means that i don't get to decide how reconciliation happens and i am responsible for being informed and supporting self-determination for indigenous people as well as calls to action.

dor: i think about this a lot. i don't think privilege makes any one human a bad person. i think ignoring your privilege, defending your privilege, or refusing to understand where that privilege comes from is the problem. i have privilege because the world is fucked up. i hate the history of north america and i hate the way it's taught. i love when columbus day comes around and the internet is flooded with "fuck that guy." i think one of the best things we can do is recognize the true history and say "no thank you, you guys did that and we are not okay with it." sharing the true history, the real stories, the actual events, that is so important.

**one of the things that i've really struggled with, especially in the past year, is that in my social media feeds brown and black people are often posting links or commentary about racism or racial violence in the news but there is a kind of white silence. i have wondered why white people aren't engaging. why aren't white people angry about racism?**

ad: i think many white people are angry about racism, but white people are both consciously and unconsciously attached to power. white people are taught that our experiences are authoritative and right. when we learn to be allies, we must wake up the fact that we are actually so fucking ignorant. we're undereducated when it comes to just about anything outside of the white gaze, and we're grossly under-practiced in talking about racism.

dor: i think it stems from people feeling like if they say something, they are admitting to being racist. or they are afraid someone will ask them about it, and they don't know how to defend their point of view. people are afraid because if i were to say "black lives matter" and someone were to say "fuck you, all lives matter" and in my mind i'm like "oh yeah, i guess that's true, all lives matter." so now i'm in a place where i have no idea what to say to this person, because they are right, all lives do matter, but there is a clear imbalance and i don't know how to say that, so i end up too scared to do or say anything at all.

admittedly, i do feel resentful when white people do or say nothing at all, because of this fear you are talking about. so much of my own learning this year has been recognizing anti-black racism specifically, how different this is from my own experience as a person of colour, and my own privilege in this respect. it has been challenging and even uncomfortable at times to know how to show solidarity. but i constantly have to remind myself that being an ally is ultimately learning to be comfortable with being uncomfortable. that it's more important that i use my voice and privilege, and probably mess up along the way, than to do or say nothing.

**this has also been the year when i have been saying to white friends, it's not enough to not be racist, i need you to step up. what are examples of your allyship towards people of colour?**

sq: i've always felt that one of the most crucial things a white person must do as an ally is to listen to the voices of people of colour— essential voices that are so often marginalized and silenced in mainstream society, it sometimes takes some extra effort to hear them. in my early twenties, i moved to montreal, and it was there that the world of social justice and politics really opened up to me. so many of the writers and thinkers i admired then and now are people of colour. i was compelled to learn from diverse voices and not just accept the perspectives of mass media. bell hooks and angela davis led me to writers like james baldwin and alice walker. a dozen years later it feels even easier to find and be inspired by (new-to-me) writers like hilton als or ta-nehisi coates. and that's just writers. there is so much happening right now in music and art and on the front lines of the movement for racial justice that is being expertly and fiercely documented by people of colour. the idea of "listening" also involves being aware of what we're consuming at all times. if my tastes become too homogenous—in music, art, or literature—i actively go out and look for other stuff, to make sure that i'm hearing those diverse voices. learning from outside of a dominant white culture has truly enriched my life. and hopefully it has made me a better ally too.

dor: i think sharing stories, articles, essays, videos from the point of view of people of colour is such a strong and easy way to contribute to a positive dialogue. i always try to share a good solid tweet, video, or write-up from a person of colour because i think it's important that those creators have the opportunity to create even more. i could retweet a white guy who says "racism ruins lives" or i could retweet a muslim guy who is saying "racism is ruining my life." that story is more powerful, real, true, and the perspective is what matters. i think (as with all movements) you need people from all sides standing up with/for you, but it's important that the movement originates within that community.

rs: the only way to support folks when you have more privilege is to give power away (which means space, money/resources, and time). i run a record label and put on a lot of the shows. when i'm looking at who i should play with or support artistically, i try to give space, resources, and time to gender minorities, queer folks, and/or people of colour.

ad: it's a bit of an abstract example, however i continually remind myself that getting involved is not about becoming a "good white person." people of colour are in no way obliged to see or acknowledge any of my humble learning moments or acts of allyship. it's not about "saving white face" to evade the reality of my own part in perpetuating racism. allyship is gradual, delicate, challenging, and life-long work. the work alone (not the outcomes or accomplishments) has to be and is reason enough.

> i agree. the "good white person" is a myth, one that people of colour can't afford to believe in. especially when we are seldom shown the same kind of generosity applied to our intentions—i am never perceived as a "good brown person" in conversations about racism. if anything, it's usually the opposite. what is most important and needed is a person who listens and takes action.

**the one thing you can do**
*for yi-fen chou*

use your own name
name your colour
over and over

learn its meaning
history advantage
over and over

white is not poison
just your disavowal of it
over and over.

**thank you for naming all of your privileges**

now what?

**bloody mary**
white supremacy
white supremacy
white supremacy.

the origins of skin

**prologue / gestation**

*i dreamt i lay on my belly and our creator fascia cut into my lower*
*back with arms shaped like large copper scissors*

*sliced along my spine to the top of my head painless*
*she unwrapped me from my skin her arm blades now blunt*

*unzipped from this cloak i awaited cold but instead a benevolent*
*heat the kind i had known in my childhood when we lived on land*

*together she and i stretched out my skin my flayed fists*
*pounded it flat her tongue rolled it smooth we examined it*

*our fingers and eyes anchored on my exterior the physical*
*map others read to navigate me*

*borders meridians markings not of my making*
*who knew hue could be so divisive? she whispered*

do you see now? your skin is evil
*afflicted we both turned away had to*

*you appeared when we were not*
*looking robed yourself in my skin.*

*you smirked.*
            *she shrugged.*
                        *frost formed.*

**one / birth**

would you believe me if I told you the purpose of skin
                                    is not utility but unity?

you had lamented *fascia! our planet is wet and cold*
                                    so I wove a fabric

especially for you all of you it had to be new unlike any fabric
                                    that had existed before

i wove nothing into something just the motion of my hands weaving
                                    my hands weaving created skin

i had spawned and spun many beautiful creations but human
                                    skin its sensitivity elasticity

made me wish for my own i didn't know then how complex
                                    an organ skin would become

as it grew skin spread over my knee and descended a

w

a

t

e

r

f

a

l

l

i marvelled then wrapped you in it i wanted you to feel
close to me less alone

so I made your skin the colour of my home the night sky
you were already stars

**two / childhood**

your word *skin* derived from your word *sky*
dark and illimitable

      invincible

now that weather couldn't touch you
as before

      wide-eyed

discovering new gifts your planet offered
you cultivated

      land

braved the sun learned to swim
touched your bodies

tongue

tug tuck taste trace throat thrust trust
the first

time

you said the word *my* followed by *skin*
you felt nearest and furthest from

me.

## three / adolescence

before skin
you only looked
at each other
with purest love

raw hands pressed

over your rib
cage in case
your heart tried
to jump out

what was that like?

remember when
last you looked
at something
someone

without attaching

*want*
but rather
an irrepressible
satisfaction

in their existence?

**four / adulthood**

with skin came shape no longer amorphous distinction another gift
your curiosity did not last
twisted quickly into contrast

you told yourself new myths of superiority solely based
on your exteriority fabricated
the idea of *flaw*

said *i feel less than* and to justify your sense of lack
you cut holes
in your body

as you would later cut holes in your own earth as though
no home can hold you
no home can whole you

let your blood drain out then took the blood of others and took and took
this is how your skin
lost its colour

tragedy of the human body: once given you disembodied
first yourselves then each other
blaming me—*for fascia!*

maybe skin was a mistake you were better off uncovered astral
maybe bodies are inconsolable
irreconcilable

or maybe you confused desire for deficiency born from touch
my hands weaving it is always touch
embrace that you crave

this is the secret of skin
restoration begins with extending and
the end of taking.

**epilogue / decomposition**

*freedom: the ability to name something bad about yourself*
*outside yourself*
*dark*

*dark past dark secret dark tale dark truth*
*naming something*
*dark*

*affirms what remains of you is light is right is free what happens*
*when they mark the entirety of you as*
*dark*

*that is how they named me there can be no light*
*for me even when my*
*dark*

*body stands naked beneath the midday sun no way to right me no*
*redemption*
*no freedom i cannot leave this*
*darkness*

*behind like the past hide*
*it like a secret*
*darkness*

*is my tale my truth and this truth of me is always here and so i'm always*
*the bad about you*
*outside of you.*

**brown dreams**

*i do not believe we will win. i do not believe hope should be a prerequisite for trying anyways.*

—alok vaid-menon

**call in sick**

how many mornings
        don't
        count

how many mornings
        fresh slate sun rays hope
        eclipsed by reminder of your own body

how many mornings
        does it storm without storming
        do you feel eaten but don't feel like eating

how many mornings
        log in refresh dodge comments
        scan comments log out restart

how many mornings
       tally likes for love wonder what a click tap
       from a stranger grants you that you can't grant
       yourself what the lack of a click tap takes
       from you that you can't give yourself

how many mornings
       google *toronto tallest bridges subway suicides*
       "only 60 percent who jump die"

how many mornings
       *you have run out of sick days*
       when do you run out of being brown?

**often brown feels like *but***

*conjunction*
> 1. used to introduce something contrasting with what has already been mentioned
> 2. used to indicate the impossibility of anything other than what is being stated
> 3. used to introduce a response expressing a feeling such as surprise or anger

*preposition*
> 1. except; apart from; other than

*adverb*
> 1. no more than; only

*noun*
> 1. an argument against something; an objection.

## how to not disappoint you completely

if i write about you is it           appropriation
if i don't write about you is it     erasure
if i include you is it              tokenizing
if i don't include you is it        invisibilizing

will you say *perpetuating*       *pandering*
*centering neoliberal*           *homonormative*
*capitalist individualist narcissist*   *selfish*
*only interested in being*        *famous*

if i am learning should i        know better
if i err am i                    failure
if i list my privileges am i      accountable
if i ask these questions am i    responsible
when i apologize will i be        forgiven.

**when i feel jealous**

whiteness the meteor that fractured our planet shattered
us apart our memories erased brown fragments unanchored
in white space

this is why every time a brown person sees another brown
person—a double take *do i know you?* in my dreams
we clutch each other

praise each other desperate to reconnect but when i wake
i am jealous of you how much white people like you
or maybe all this time

i have been aching for you to remember me to remember you
as intimate instead of adversary so *how can i love you better?*
what i ask myself

when i feel jealous won't let        scarcity        come between
we have already lost so much
when we should be friends.

**omar**

struck by two the night i saw you first—
your brashness how you danced like your body
was performing an original cover of each song
second—the perma pucker-shape of your lips

searched for you on facebook success
(never more grateful for mutual friends feature)
scrolled your photos studying your poses arms tattoos
*i'm-the-shit* captions like scripture patch of chest hair
you flaunted deep v necks only reminded me
of my own the one i hid waxed clearing a path
for pimples to bloom

you were a model—of course—but it wasn't just your beauty
it was your sexy how you knew named owned your fuckability
was this allowed for brown boys? yesterday i forced myself
to watch aziz having sex on *master of none* listen
to him moan not cringe but absorb
a brown body having giving pleasure

*you can't love anyone until you love yourself*
i have found the opposite to be true
you a reflection the brown mirror
i never had a face to look upon
adore when mine was ugly my selfie
pre-selfie

when we met—finally—you confessed
you had posted on tumblr about wanting me
to do something dirty to you
i giggled blushed
you apologized.

**under the pink**

if i could tunnel back
        through time
aggression
        dead skin cells
i would guard
        all my softness
my tender places
        like my life
depended on it
        so that when
i grew up
        i wouldn't feel
i had lost
        everything.

**muscle**

pledged my flesh to iron

when soft wasn't safe
muscle to make masc

masc to make muscle
muscle to mask muffle

firm instead of supple
stubble instead of smooth

in rubble my woman refused

to buckle rumbled stayed subtle
chewed out leather muzzle

i would rather trouble
struggle rather a fist

ten knuckles than cede
one more vessel to men.

**agnostic**

sometimes
the inconceivable:

i am tender
tensionless
in my body
my gender

photographs
don't make me
shrink
feel stranger

wish to be a stranger
*failure*
the word
forgotten

*cower*
the action
now a strut sway
saunter

is this just because
in my bed
there is
a white man?

the first time
we kissed
my nose bled
and the second.

## skeptic

once i loved a brown woman
you said i hated myself

now i also love a white man
you say i hate myself.

### vishvarupa

you will never grasp
clasp my power

voltage to resist persist coexist
shapeshift conductor for your spark

my skin is brown
to caution you of my fire.

**how many books have to be written?**

two hundred thousand years
of human life

fire flight language music wheel
architecture vaccine electricity

one five ten fifteen twenty years
from now another brown person

stares at white screen glare
types the word race

five billion years
until the sun dies.

## brown dreams

how often must you prove your pigment
when your entire body is painted bronze

have you ever heard white question its colour
snow moon salt milk tooth chalk

what if there is no right way to be brown
besides the brown you are

soil nut clove wheat bark pluto.

**author's note**

as a non-black person of colour writing a book about racism, i felt it necessary to acknowledge anti-black racism. my hope is that this comes through in this book.

i also felt it necessary to consider what it means to be given a platform to discuss racism while being a settler in canada, where indigenous people have faced and continue to face racial violence, and the dismissal of this violence.

as a small gesture of gratitude for living on indigenous land, the traditional territory of the mississaugas of new credit first nation, i am donating half of my author royalties for this book to the **native youth sexual health network** (nyshn), "an organization by and for indigenous youth that works across issues of sexual and reproductive health, rights and justice throughout the united states and canada."

## sources

my writing practice for this book consisted of consuming a lot of poetry.
below is a list of books by black and indigenous authors,
and authors of colour that were particularly inspiring:

*the black unicorn: poems*, audre lorde
*citizen: an american lyric*, claudia rankine
*for your own good*, leah horlick
*kiyâm*, naomi mcilwraith
*seva*, sharanpal ruprai
*salt*, nayyirah waheed

**epigraph**
ahmed, sara. "a phenomenology of whiteness." *feminist theory* 8 no. 2 (2007): 149–68.

**white dreams**
koul, scaachi. "can tv make us not hate ourselves?" *buzzfeed* october 14, 2015.

**indian**
partly inspired by teddy syrette quoted in francis, margot. "from decolonizing the emotions to de-colonizing the nation ... affective challenges in theatre re-membering indigenous claims to land in canada." *this is indian land*, karl hele, ed., (winnipeg, mb: aboriginal issues press, 2016).

**amiskwacîwâskahikan**
spelling of amiskwacîwâskahikan (cree word for edmonton) from creedictionary.com.

**yellowface**
found poem based on michael derrick hudson (as yi-fen chou), "biography," in *the best american poetry 2015*, lehmen, david, and sherman alexie, eds. (new york, ny: scribner, 2015).

**what pride looked like june 24, 2015**
based on events at lgbt pride reception at the white house on june 24, 2015.

**#oscars2016**
found poem based on comments in interviews made by charlotte rampling (*the guardian*), michael caine (bbc), julie delpy (*the wrap*), clint eastwood (tmz.com), and kristin stewart (variety)
poem alludes to #oscarssowhite, created by april reign (reignofapril.com).

**54,216 signed petition to ban kanye west from playing pan am games closing ceremony**
found poem based on comments on change.org petition "don't have kanye west head-line the closing ceremony for the toronto pan american games" july 2015.

**miley, what's good?**
found poem based on coscarelli, joe. "miley cyrus on nicki minaj and hosting a 'raw' mtv video music awards." *the new york times* august 27, 2015.

**how to talk to a white person**
gay, roxanne. "the charge to be fair: a conversation with ta-nehisi coates" *barnes & noble review* august 10, 2015.

**a dog named lavender**
diangelo, robin. "white fragility: why it's so hard to talk to white people about racism." *the good men project* april 9, 2015.

**brown dreams**
vaid-menon, alok. "confessional" returnthegayze.com july 15, 2015.

**often brown feels like *but***
definition of "but" from google.

**how to not disappoint you completely**
title references radiohead song title "how to disappear completely."

**under the pink**
titled after tori amos album *under the pink.*

**thank you**

brian lam & arsenal pulp press
(for believing in my work over and over again)

amber dawn
(for planting the idea of poetry)

shemeena shraya adam holman trisha yeo leah horlick maureen
hynes farzana doctor katherine friesen karen campos castillo daniel
zomparelli amy crowley margot francis shani mootoo george elliott clarke
d'bi.young anitafrika rollie pemberton sara quin rae spoon dannielle
owens-reid zoe todd rinaldo walcott kim katrin milan fonna seidu m mclean
shane rhodes dani couture christopher nicholson amar wahab alejandro
santiago oliver mcpartlin cynara geissler susan safyan robert ballantyne
mom dad shamik

this project has been generously supported by the ontario arts council
(through writers' reserve grants from bookthug, dundurn press, mawenzi
house, tightrope books, wolsak & wynn) and the toronto arts council.

grateful to the fearless indigenous and black women and women of colour
forever on the frontlines of change.

**white dreams single**

with the purchase of *even this page is white*
you have access to download the accompanying single
*white dreams*

available at: vivekshraya.com/white-dreams-single

lyrics and vocals: vivek shraya

produced and mixed by james bunton
mastered by heather kirby

photo by alejandro santiago
artwork by karen campos castillo